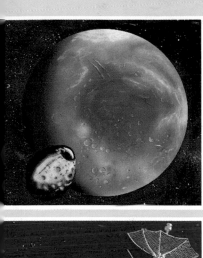

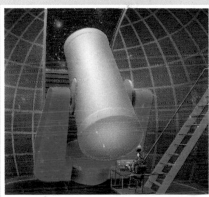
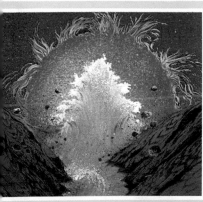

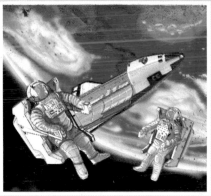

TABLE OF CONTENTS

IMAGES
Space

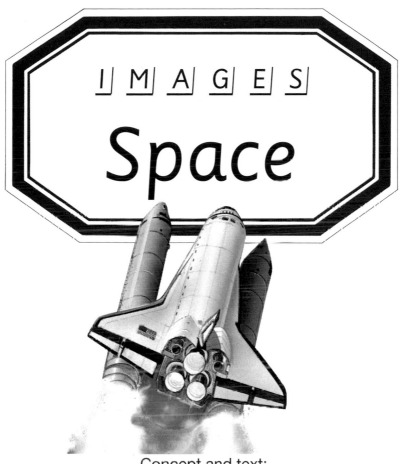

Concept and text:
Émilie Beaumont
Marie-Renée Pimont,
primary school teacher

Illustrations:
S. Alloy, P. Bon, N. Le Guillouzic,
Y. Lequesne, T. Pepperday

Translation:
Lara M. Andahazy

FLEURUS

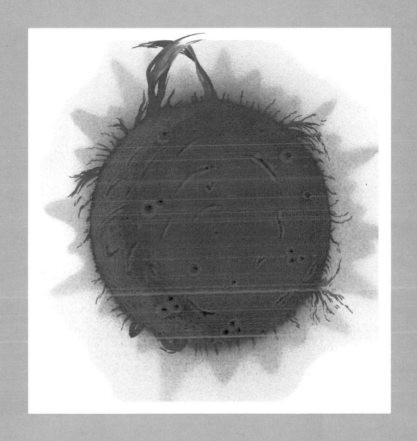

THE SOLAR SYSTEM

THE BIG BANG

The universe began with a huge explosion. Scientists have named it "the Big Bang."

We think the Big Bang took place fifteen billion years ago. After the explosion, it was very hot. Then everything cooled down and tiny balls filled the universe little by little.

These balls moved around for millions of years and bumped into each other. They formed clouds of gas and dust.

The gas and dust heated up and became the first stars which, little by little, gathered together in huge groups called galaxies.

Ten billion years ago, a bright light lit up a corner of our galaxy, the Milky Way. This is when our sun was born.

After the Big Bang, new stars were born in the galaxies and then exploded, setting free huge amounts of gas and dust which become new stars in turn.

In our galaxy, dust was attracted to the sun and began to spin very fast. This dust created larger and larger clumps that eventually formed planets.

Now, nine planets travel around the sun. Our planet, Earth, is one of these. There might be another planet like ours in other galaxies.

TRAVELING AROUND THE SUN

Nine planets travel around our sun. They make up our solar system.

This picture shows the different paths that each planet takes in its trip around the sun.

Each planet takes a different length of time to move around the sun. The planets closest to the sun are the fastest.

Can you spot Earth? It is the small blue planet near the sun.

THE NINE PLANETS

The planets in our solar system are all different sizes. The picture below shows all of them from the closest to the sun to the furthest from the sun.

They are: Mercury, Venus, Earth (the blue planet), Mars, Jupiter, Saturn, Uranus, Neptune and Pluto.

The word planet means "voyager." This was the name astrologers gave to the heavenly bodies that move all the time.

Your turn!
Point to the planet closest to the sun and say its name. Next, point to the furthest from the sun. Where is the biggest? the smallest?

THE SUN IS VERY BIG

The distance from the center of the sun to its surface is twice as long as the distance from Earth to the moon.

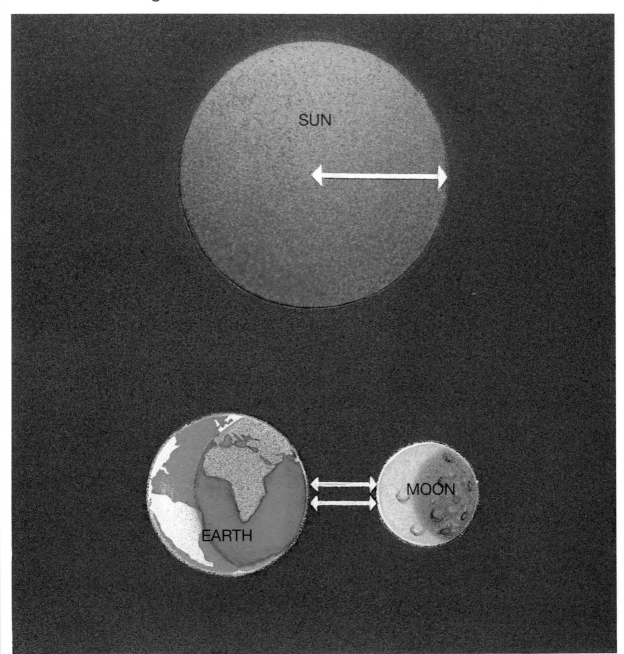

The moon is 240,000 miles from the earth! That's very far! Just imagine how big the sun is.

THE SUN

And now here's the sun. It is a large star that has been burning non-stop for billions of years.

Be careful! Never look directly at the sun. You could damage your eyes even if you're wearing sunglasses.

If you want to look at the sun, you should look through a piece of glass that a grown-up has helped you blacken with a candle.

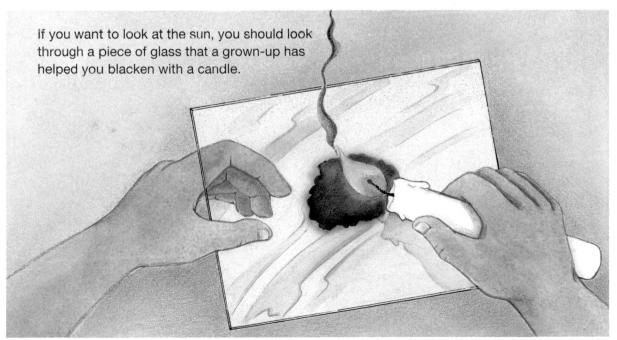

A CLOSER LOOK AT THE SUN

The surface of the sun looks like a giant grapefruit that constantly wiggles and spits flames like a dragon!

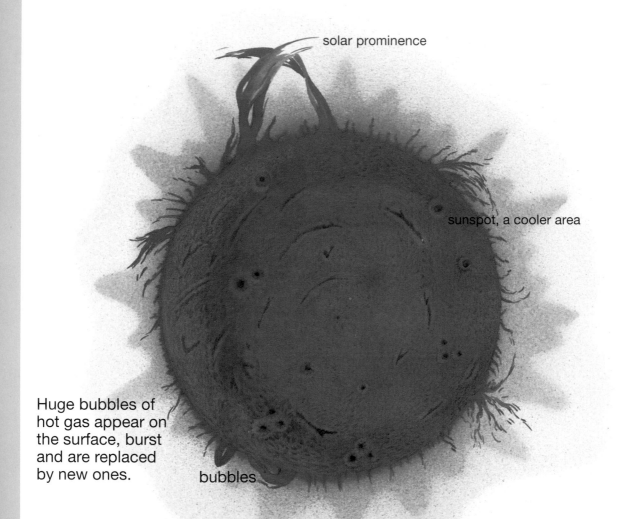

solar prominence

sunspot, a cooler area

Huge bubbles of hot gas appear on the surface, burst and are replaced by new ones.

bubbles

The center of the sun is very hot—more than 60 million degrees Fahrenheit. Can you imagine that?! It's much hotter than an oven.

Huge explosions spit gas out thousands of miles. It falls back to the surface in the form of huge flames called solar prominences.

THE DEATH OF THE SUN

The sun was born 4 billion years ago! It will continue to burn its gases for 5 billion years until it uses up all its reserves.

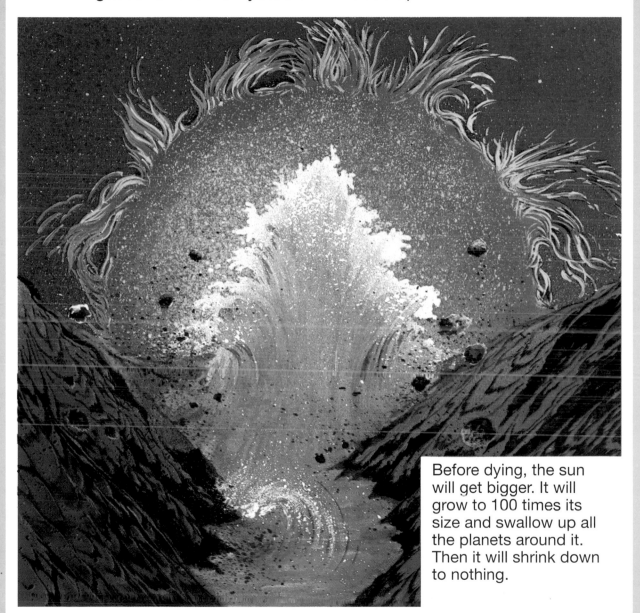

Before dying, the sun will get bigger. It will grow to 100 times its size and swallow up all the planets around it. Then it will shrink down to nothing.

When the sun gets closer to the earth, it will get unbearably hot and everything will burn up. But by then mankind will certainly have moved to safety on other planets in another galaxy.

BLACK HOLES

Like the sun will someday, other stars have already grown to huge sizes before dying. Then they became tiny and disappeared.

When a star shrinks, something mysterious happens in its center. It becomes a black hole and gravity pulls everything near it—spacecraft, rockets, rocks and even light—to the center.

MOVING PLANETS

The sun is so big that it attracted nine planets. These planets spin very quickly so that they don't fall into the sun.

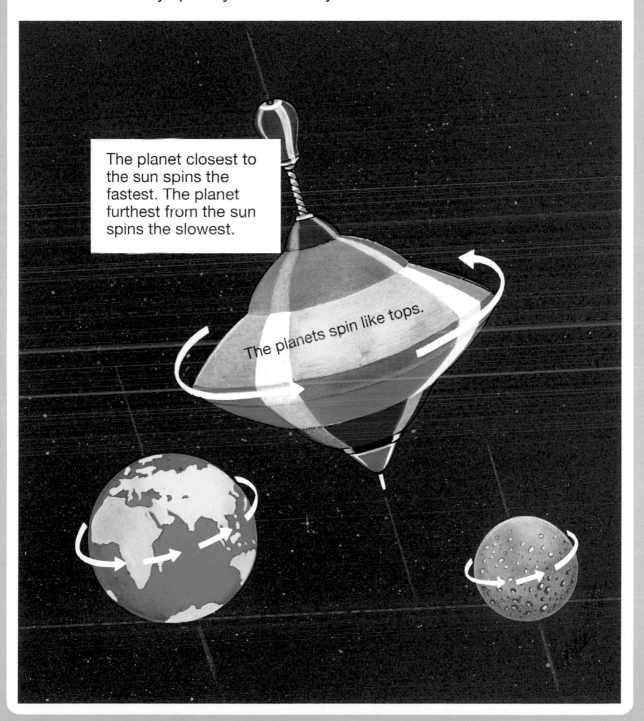

The planet closest to the sun spins the fastest. The planet furthest from the sun spins the slowest.

The planets spin like tops.

NORTHERN LIGHTS – SOUTHERN LIGHTS

The penguins below live at the South Pole. They are watching the Southern Lights called aurora australis. Eskimos that live at the North Pole can see the Northern Lights (aurora borealis).

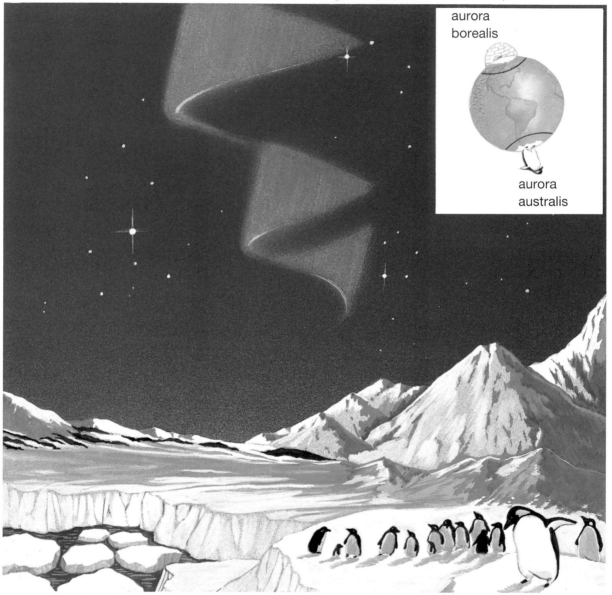

The auroras are beautiful colored lights caused by dust spit out by the sun. They can be seen in the night sky.

THE SUN AND THE EARTH

Life on Earth is possible because of the sun and water. But everything could change if there were a little more or less sunlight.

If the sun sent us less heat, entire countries would be covered in ice. This would be a street in Montreal, Canada— way too cold to go for a walk. Burrrr!

But if the sun sent us more heat, the ice at the Poles would melt and the level of oceans and rivers would rise all over the world.

QUICK QUESTIONS

Listen to each question and see if you can think
of the answer.

Is the sun
a star or
a planet?

Can we see the
aurora borealis at
the North or the
South Pole?

Is our galaxy
called the "Milky
Way" or the "Silky
Way"?

If you can answer these questions on the first try, you already know a lot. Bravo!

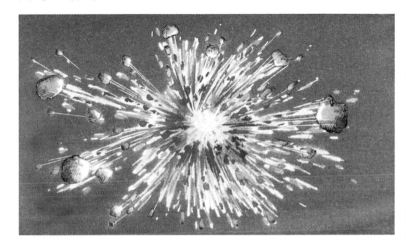

What do we call the explosion that created the universe?

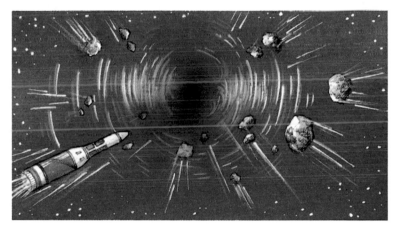

What would happen if a rocket flew too close to a black hole?

Which of these three planets—Venus, Saturn or Pluto—has rings?

ODD NORTHERN LIGHTS

This young Eskimo is watching the Northern Lights. Can you find 5 things that don't belong at the North Pole?

LETTER HUNT

Below are VENUS, EARTH, SATURN and MARS. Each planet has lost a letter. Put these four letters in the right places: R, A, U, T.

VEN_S

EA_TH

SA_URN

M_RS

NEAR AND FAR

Below are pictures of the sun as it appears to different planets. Point to each picture of the sun, starting with the smallest and ending with the biggest.

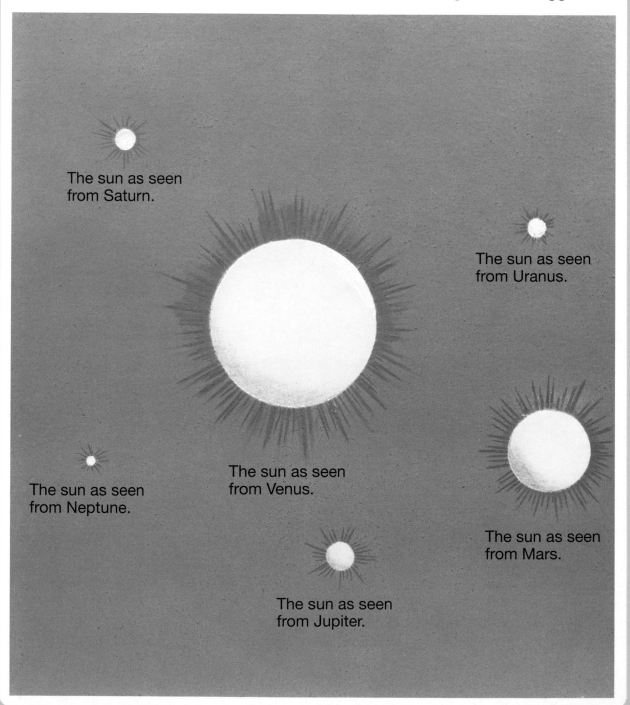

The sun as seen from Saturn.

The sun as seen from Uranus.

The sun as seen from Neptune.

The sun as seen from Venus.

The sun as seen from Mars.

The sun as seen from Jupiter.

THE PLANETS

MERCURY

This is Mercury, the planet closest to the sun. Mercury is half the size of Earth but weighs more.

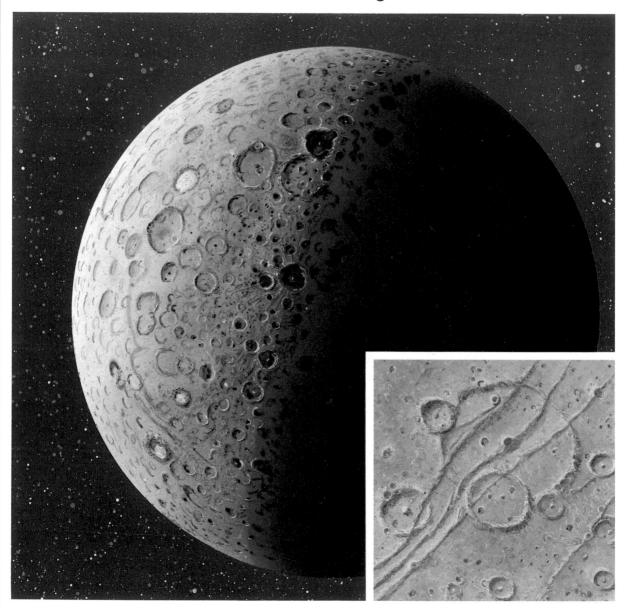

One side of Mercury is always lit by the sun. The other is always in the dark. It can be close to 800°F in the daytime.
That's very hot!

Mercury's surface is covered by craters. Large rocks fell from the sky and landed very hard because there is no air to slow their fall.

One day on Mercury is as long as 59 days on Earth. One year on Mercury is 88 Earth days long. It is hard to see Mercury because it is so close to the sun which blinds us.

VENUS

Venus is sometimes called the "Shepherd's Star" even though it is not a star. It only shines when the sun lights it up.

You can see Venus on summer nights when it is time for shepherds to bring in their sheep.

Venus is almost the same size as Earth. It has mountains and volcanoes. It is very hot. Venus is covered by a thick layer of clouds.

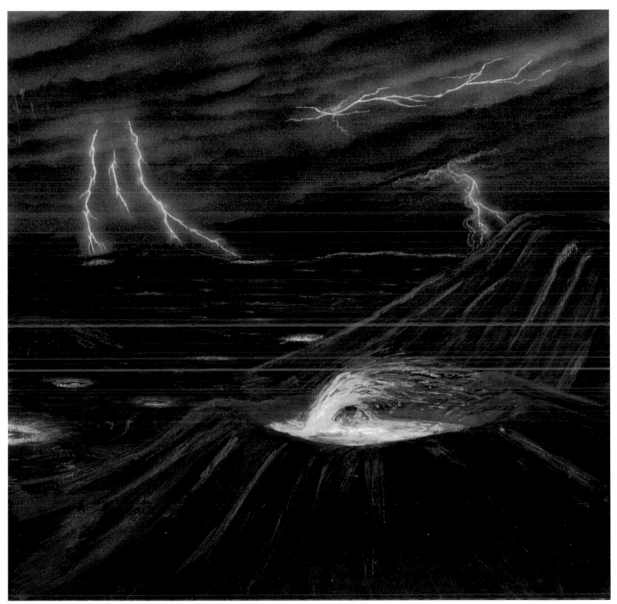

It is dark and very hot on the surface of Venus. Even metal would melt there. Lightening storms break all the time. One day on Venus is as long as 243 days on Earth. One Venus year is 224 Earth days long. One day lasts more than a year!

EARTH

Here are pictures of both sides of our planet, Earth. Do you know why it is called the "blue planet"?

This is because most of planet Earth is covered by oceans. Astronauts can see your home country in the middle of all this blue from outer space.

ANOTHER LOOK AT EARTH

Can you find the different oceans and continents under the clouds that surround Earth? Can you see your home country?

Every day satellites send pictures like these to meteorologists. They use them to predict rain or sunny weather by watching the way the clouds move.

THE BEGINNING OF LIFE ON EARTH

Life began a billion years after our planet was formed.
It all began at the bottom of the oceans.

In the beginning, Earth was
a huge ball of molten rock.

Then it cooled down
and clouds formed.

Next, rain fell and filled
the oceans and seas.

Plants developed because of
the sun and water.

If we compare the earth to man, it is huge. But if we compare it to the universe, our planet is no bigger than a grain of sand.

Plants covered the earth little by little.

Then the first animals—dinosaurs—appeared.

Monkeys and apes appeared 30 million years ago.

Men have existed for 3 million years.

OUR SPINNING EARTH

The earth spins around once every 24 hours (one day).
When it is day on one side it is night on the other.

You can see the sun rise in the east in the morning
and set in the west in the evening.

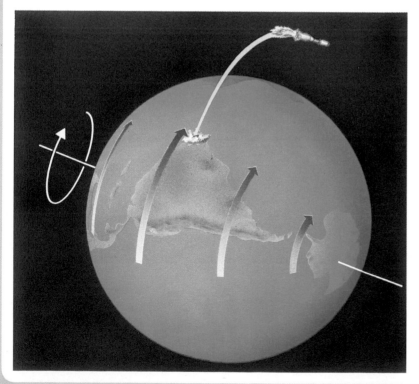

Rockets need to fly very fast in order to leave the layer of air that surrounds Earth.

A VOYAGE AROUND THE SUN

It takes Earth 365 days to go around the sun once.
This is one year with four different seasons.

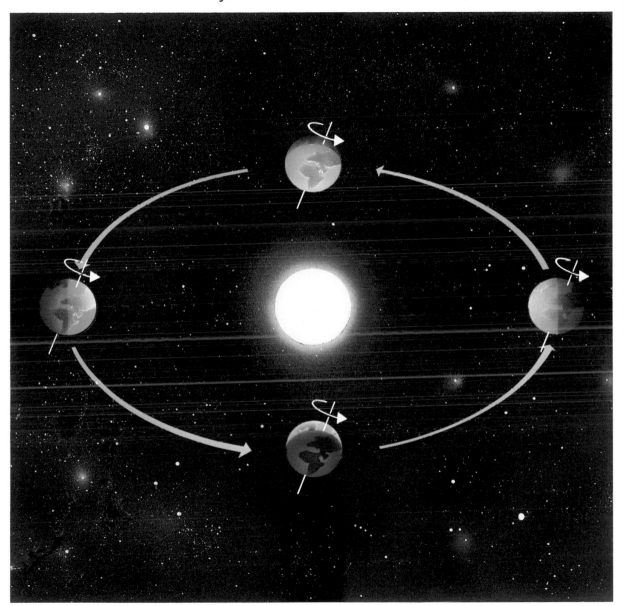

Follow the earth's path with your finger. Start on the right. This is where our planet is in winter. Next comes spring, summer and finally autumn at the bottom of the picture.

MARS

Reddish in color, Mars is roughly the same size as
Earth but it is further from the sun than we are.

Two small satellites or moons move around Mars. They are called
Phobos and Deimos. You can see one in front of Mars. The other
is to the left and behind Mars. It is tiny.

On Mars there is no water and we can't breathe the air there.
Days are the same length as days on Earth
but one year on Mars is 687 days long.

Everything is huge on Mars. The Viking space probe sent by the
United States found mountains twice as tall as any on Earth
and canyons twice as deep!

JUPITER AND ITS MOONS

Jupiter is a giant planet 1,500 times the size of Earth.
One year on Jupiter is 12 Earth years long.

This planet is the largest in our solar system. It has 16 moons,
4 of which are very big! You can see the surface of one of
Jupiter's moons, Io, and its erupting volcanoes in the picture
above.

Astronomers discovered a red spot on the surface of Jupiter. It is thought to be caused by a huge storm! Can you find the red spot near the bottom of the picture?

The surface we see is made up of clouds.

solid core

The planet Jupiter is made up of a solid core surrounded by gases and clouds. We can not land on the surface of the planet because our rockets would sink in the clouds!

SATURN

The planet Saturn is known for its beautiful rings.
It is nine times the size of Earth.

23 moons rotate around Saturn. The largest, Titan, is surrounded by fog. It is –292°F on its surface. That's very, very cold! Just think, water freezes at +32°F.

Saturn is made up of gases and is so light it could float on an ocean—if we could find one big enough for this giant planet!

Saturn is surrounded by thousands of very bright rings made up of chunks of ice and rock. These different sized chunks spin around Saturn at top speed.

URANUS, NEPTUNE AND PLUTO

Oh! how far we are from the sun. The last three planets
are giant Neptune, Uranus and tiny Pluto.

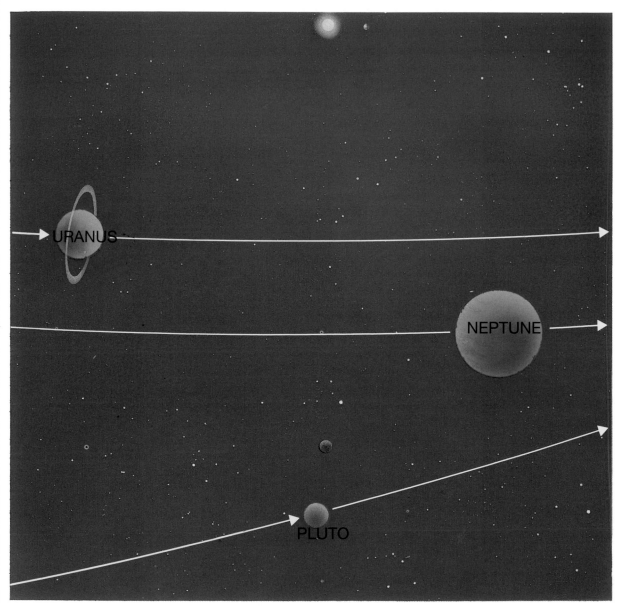

Uranus has rings around it. We first discovered them not very
long ago. It would take a rocket 20 years to fly to Neptune. No
bigger than the moon, Pluto is almost 4 billion miles from the sun!

THE DAYS OF THE WEEK

In the old days, astronomers only knew about five planets and the moon. In many different languages the days of the week are named after these planets.

In English, Monday means the day of the moon and Saturday the day of Saturn. In other languages, French for example, Tuesday was named for Mars, Wednesday for Mercury, Thursday for Jupiter and Friday for Venus.

ONE MONTH OR ONE YEAR?

Once you know what makes one month and what makes a year, you'll see that we live by the rhythms of the universe!

One **month** equals the time it takes the **moon** to go around the **earth** once.

One **year** equals the time it takes the **earth** to go around the **sun** once.

A PLANET A DAY

You saw that the days of the week were named after the planets in different languages. Can you match the planets and their days?

MONDAY

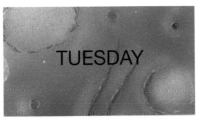
TUESDAY

WEDNESDAY

MERCURY   JUPITER   VENUS

MOON   SATURN   MARS

THURSDAY   FRIDAY   SATURDAY

49

HAPPY BIRTHDAY!

In the beginning of the chapter you saw that the planets all take different amounts of time to move around the sun.

Saturn takes 30 Earth years to make its trip. One Saturn year equals 30 Earth years. One Uranus year is 84 Earth years long.

These three people are all one year old today. One lives on Earth, one on Saturn and one on Uranus. Who is one Earth year old? Who is one Saturn year old? Who is one Uranus year old?

WHAT A FUNNY SKY!

Sarah is looking at the night sky. It is filled with funny things.
How many can you find?

A DAY IN THE LIFE OF BENJAMIN

What is Benjamin doing in each of the pictures on the right?
Point out the position of the sun during each activity.

The sun is rising.
It is morning.

Benjamin is playing ball.

The sun is high in the sky.
It is early afternoon.

Benjamin is getting up.

The sun is setting.
It is evening.

Benjamin is closing his shutters
before going to bed.

AN ACCIDENT IN OUTER SPACE

These three planets have broken in two! Can you put them back together? What are their names?

TRUE OR FALSE

For each sentence, remember what you've learned and say if it is true or false.

(1) VENUS is closer to the sun than EARTH. TRUE or FALSE?

(2) MARS is the planet furthest from the sun. TRUE or FALSE?

(3) JUPITER is the biggest planet in the solar system. TRUE or FALSE?

(4) EARTH moves
around the sun
in one day.
TRUE or FALSE?

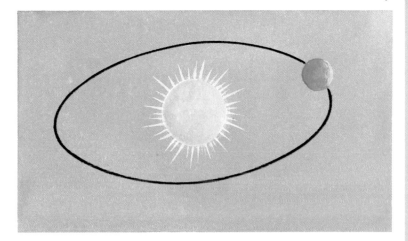

(5) SATURDAY
means the day of
MERCURY.
TRUE or FALSE?

Mercury

Venus

Earth

(6) EARTH is also
called the
blue planet.
TRUE or FALSE?

A SNACK FROM OUTER SPACE

With a little help, you can make a delicious space snack for your friends. Wouldn't it be fun to eat moons, stars and planets?!

Star and Moon Cookies:
1 3/4 cup flour
2/3 cup sugar
1/2 cup butter
2 egg yolks
the juice from 1 lemon

Put all the ingredients in a big bowl and mix well. Use a rolling pin to roll out the dough and cut out stars and moons with cookie cutters. Bake them in the oven on low heat for 20 minutes.

Marzipan Planets

You can even add a few drops of vanilla extract.

You need 3/4 cups sugar, 2 tablespoons flour and 3 tablespoons butter.

Mix all the ingredients in a large bowl. Then make small balls for the planets. They are ready to eat!

Now you're ready to lay out your stars, moons and planets on a large tray covered in crinkly aluminum foil. Enjoy!

star stickers to decorate cups

different colored candies

star and moon candle holders

DRAW A NEW PLANET

Since no one has ever seen the planets in other galaxies
you can have fun imagining them.

The illustrator had fun drawing two funny planets. How many
different shapes can you dream up?

Look at this bird planet.
Isn't it funny?!

Use paper and crayons to invent
your own planets.

STARS AND
GALAXIES

WATCHING THE UNIVERSE

Scientists that observe the universe are called "astronomers."
They dream of finding new planets and stars!

Astronomers work in observatories. These are often built on mountain tops where the air is pure. In low areas, the light from cities and dust makes it hard to see the stars clearly.

AN OPEN ROOF

Observatory roofs open up and computers control the movement of the telescopes.

It is night and this astronomer has opened the observatory roof. He is using his telescope to study the planets, stars and galaxies. He also takes photos using his telescope.

YOU CAN BE AN ASTRONOMER TOO

You too can watch the stars and the moon with a telescope. The night sky is even more beautiful through a telescope!

Choose a clear night with lots of stars to see. With a telescope you can even see the craters of the moon (see the picture on page 84). You might need the help of a grown-up because telescopes are often hard to focus.

WHAT A LONG TIME AGO!

Mankind has always observed the night sky. We have learned a lot about how the universe works over the ages.

a temple that was used as an observatory

The Mayas in Central America built observatories a very, very long time ago. They even knew about the planet Venus but they thought it brought bad luck.

In prehistoric times, men lined up huge stones called menhirs
or standing stones. Below is a picture of Stonehenge
in England.

Some scientists think it was used to study the movement of the sun
and stars. These huge blocks of stone were put in place 5,000 years
ago! We still wonder how they managed to lift these huge stones.

ROUND OR FLAT

We didn't always agree on the shape of Earth. Some said it was round while others said it was flat.

Some people used to think that the earth was the center of the universe and that the sun and other planets moved around it.

Others thought that the earth was a flat disk that floated inside a hollow ball. For them, the sun and stars were attached to the sides of the ball.

THE MILKY WAY

Have you seen a bright white veil amongst the stars on a moonless night? It is called the Milky Way.

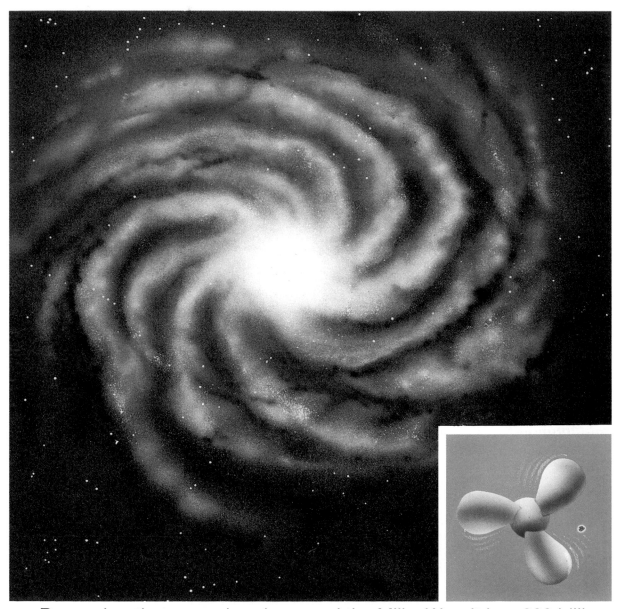

Remember that our galaxy is named the Milky Way. It has 200 billion stars in it! This is what it looks like from the outside. It looks like a giant spinning propeller floating in the universe.

THE SHAPES OF GALAXIES

The Milky Way, which looks like a propeller, is called a spiral galaxy.
But galaxies come in many different shapes.

Here is a galaxy that looks a little like ours. But it has a big bar across its middle. See it?

This galaxy is almost round. It is the most common shape for galaxies. Doesn't it look like a football?!

CONSTELLATIONS

Look at these stars. When you connect them with lines you can see shapes in the sky. These are constellations.

The five stars in the shape of a W are the constellation Cassiopeia. The ones that look like a pot with a long handle belong to the Big Dipper (it is also called Ursa Major).

THE NORTH STAR

Do you know the North Star? It is always to be found in the north. It is the brightest star in the picture on the left page.

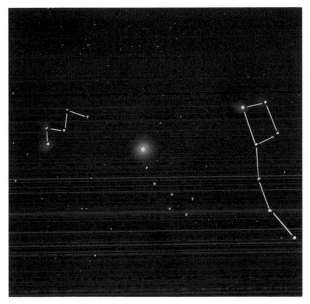 

Cassiopeia and the Big Dipper change positions around the North Star with the changing seasons. Above left is in winter; above right is in spring.

summer   winter

POLARIS

Polaris is one of the names of the North Star. It is also called Alpha Ursae Minoris! Like all stars, it twinkles in the sky.

You can check that the North Star really is in the north with a compass. Compass needles always point north.

ASTEROIDS AND METEORITES

Asteroids are chunks of rock. They can be big or small.
There is a belt of asteroids between Mars and Jupiter.

Sometimes asteroids change directions and crash into the
Earth. But you don't have to worry, this doesn't happen very
often!

SHOOTING STARS

When small asteroids change direction and enter the air around the earth they start to burn up.

These small asteroids become balls of fire. You can see them at night because they burn up in the sky before they reach the ground. We call them shooting stars.

METEORITES

When a very big asteroid crashes into Earth, it is called a meteorite. You can often see a mark left by the crash.

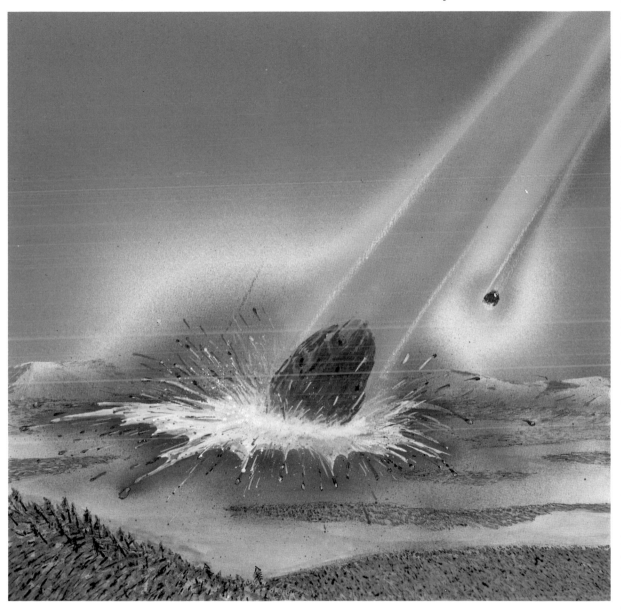

A huge ball of fire crashed to the ground in Siberia a long time ago. It burned up everything for miles around. Some scientists say that it was a meteorite.

WHAT A BIG HOLE!

Thousands of years ago a huge meteorite landed in a desert in Arizona. It left a huge crater.

Try to imagine the size of the crater! It is just under a mile wide. Ask your parents to show you just how long a mile is. Then you can tell how big the crater is.

COMETS

Comets are huge, invisible blocks of ice and dust. When they get near the sun the ice melts and a luminous streak appears.

Have you heard of Halley's Comet? It travels around the sun on a very long path. It regularly passes close by our planet. It can be seen from many parts of the world. What a beautiful sight it is!

WHICH ONE IS OUR GALAXY?

Look closely at this picture. It shows the three galaxies you have already seen. Each one is a different shape.

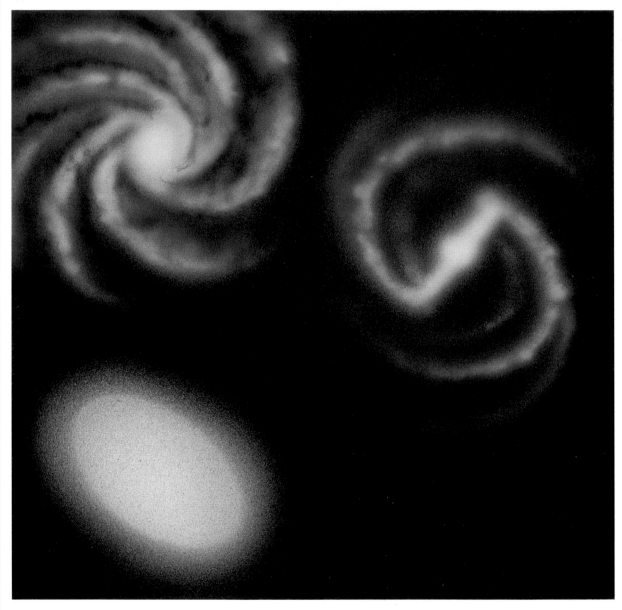

Point to the galaxy shaped like a football. What is the name of the propeller-shaped galaxy? Are there stars and planets in galaxies?

WHERE IS THE NORTH?

On starless nights you can't use the North Star to find the north
What instrument will these sailors use?

compass   spyglass   top

Today, sailors have computers on their ships and modern machines to find their way. They don't need the North Star any more.

WATCH OUT FOR METEORITES!

These four asteroids have been flying through space for a long time. One of them is going to hit the earth and become a meteorite.

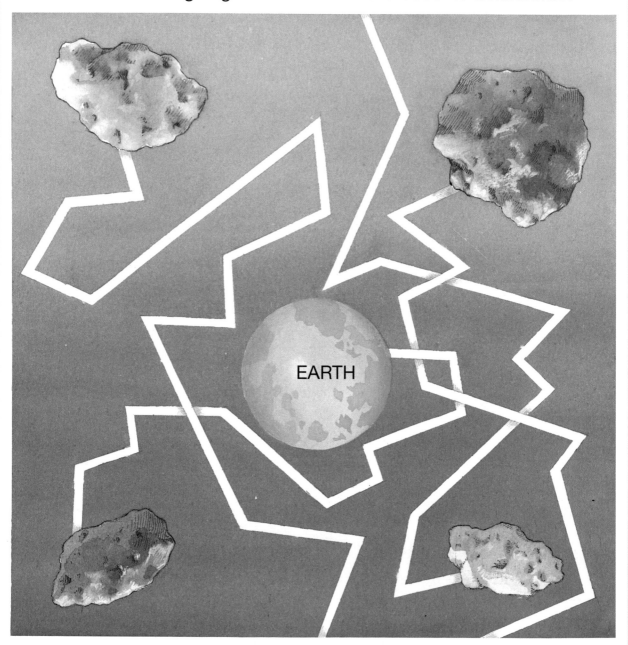

Follow the path of each asteroid with your finger. Which one is going to become a meteorite?

A NAME IN THE STARS

This little girl's name is written in the sky. Follow the letters with your finger to read her name: E - S - T - E - L - L - E.

Scientists have named the largest and brightest stars but they gave them very complicated names.

IT'S A FULL MOON TONIGHT

Two different artists drew pictures of the same countryside. But they didn't see the same things. Can you find six differences?

ODD STARS!

What a sad night for these stars! They have each lost a point or two. Can you help them find their missing points?

Do you know why stars twinkle? It's because their light has to move through the air around Earth before we can see it. The air vibrates and makes it look like the light from the stars is trembling too!

WEAR THE UNIVERSE!

You can make yourself a magician's costume with a little bit of patience and glitter, stickers and crayons.

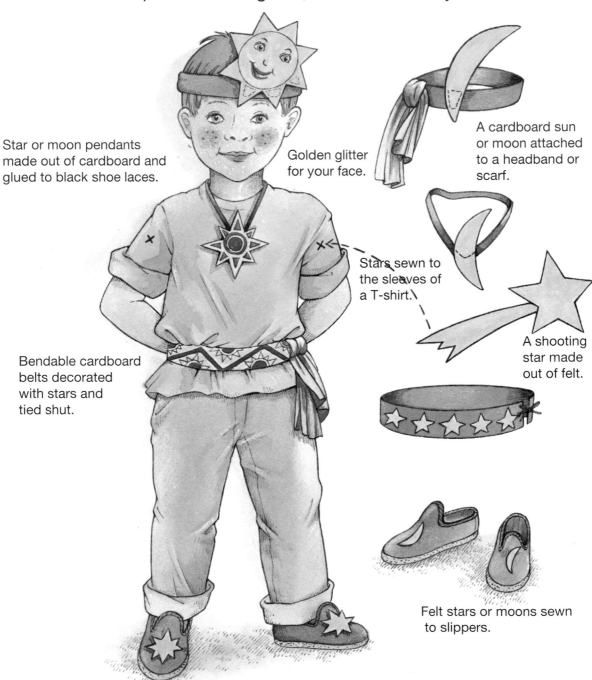

Star or moon pendants made out of cardboard and glued to black shoe laces.

Golden glitter for your face.

A cardboard sun or moon attached to a headband or scarf.

Stars sewn to the sleeves of a T-shirt.

A shooting star made out of felt.

Bendable cardboard belts decorated with stars and tied shut.

Felt stars or moons sewn to slippers.

THE MOON

LUNAR MOUNTAINS AND PLAINS

You can see the craters on the moon with a telescope.
They were made by meteorites.

crater

sea

mountain
chains

From Earth we can see darker areas called "seas." There is no water
on the moon so they are really just great plains! The lighter areas are
mountains.

THE DIFFERENT PHASES OF THE MOON

From Earth we can only see the part of the moon that is lit up by the sun. Below are the different "shapes" of the moon in a month.

1

2

3

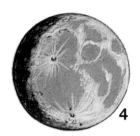

4

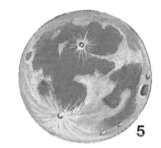

5

1. New moon: for us, the moon is black. The sun is shining on the back side of the moon. **2.** First crescent. **3.** First quarter: it looks like a D. **4.** The moon is almost full. **5.** Full moon: you can see all of it. **6.** The shadow has switched sides. **7.** Last quarter: it looks like a backwards D. **8.** Last crescent.

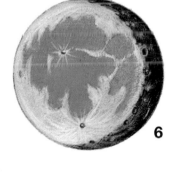

6

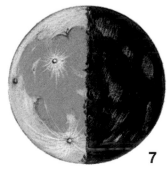

7

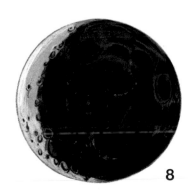

8

EARTH LIGHT

Man can admire the beautiful blue surface of Earth from the moon. It is truly a beautiful sight!

There is no wind on the moon to erase the footsteps left by astronauts.

THE MOON, EARTH'S SATELLITE

The moon is a small planet that moves around the earth
in 29 days. It is our "satellite."

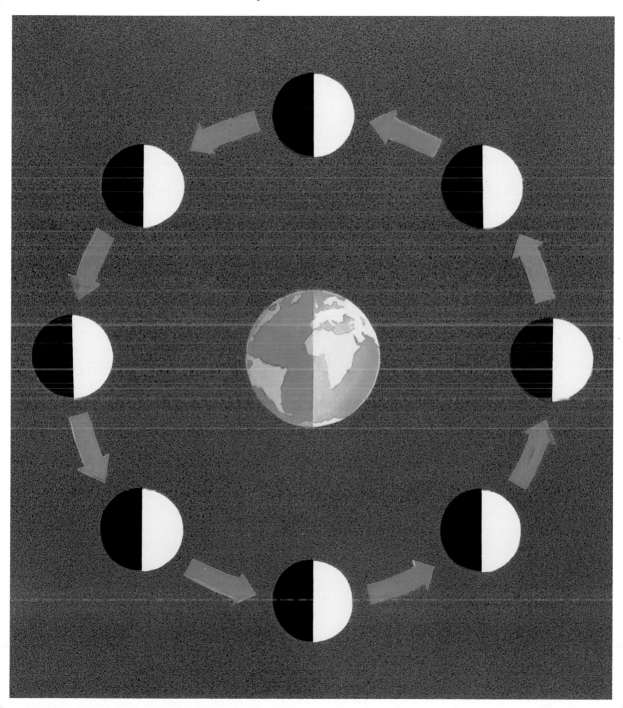

PLAYING HIDE AND SEEK WITH THE SUN!

There is a solar eclipse whenever the moon hides
the sun from us.

For a few minutes of the day in parts of the world it seems like
night. You can only see a bright ring—the edge of the sun
peeking out from behind the moon.

THE MOON AND THE OCEANS

Did you know that the moon pulls on the water in the oceans on Earth? This is what causes the tides.

The earth has turned. The moon isn't pulling as hard. The sea will move back for 6 hours. This is low tide.

Then, for 6 hours the seas move up the beaches again. This is high tide.

THE GARDENER AND THE MOON

Here is a gardener who is good friends with the moon. He knows that his garden will be better if he plants or prunes at the right times.

He plants tomatoes and flowers during the first quarter.

He plants lettuce during the full moon.

He prunes his rose bushes during the last quarter.

He plants his carrots during the last crescent.

ARE YOU A LUNATIC?

A "lunatic" is a crazy person. The word comes from the Latin for moon because the moon was thought to make people crazy. What expressions do you know with the word "moon"?

This boy is in a bad mood. In France, they say he's "got a bad moon"!

This boy wants the moon. He wants something impossible—to fly like a bird.

This girl is daydreaming. In France, they say she is "on the moon."

These newlyweds are leaving for their honeymoon.

YOUR OWN LUNAR CALENDAR

You can make your own lunar calendar by looking at the moon every night for a month, drawing what you see and writing down the date.

Ask your parents when the lunar month begins. Use a compass to draw a circle and color in the part of the moon that you can see. Tape the pages of your book together.

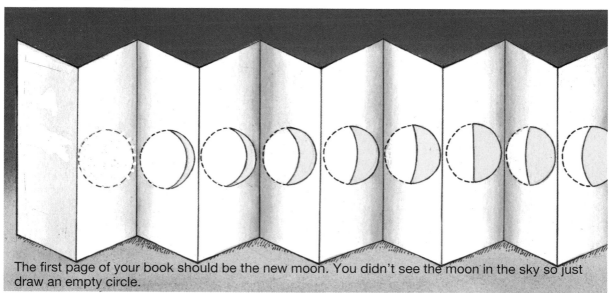

The first page of your book should be the new moon. You didn't see the moon in the sky so just draw an empty circle.

When you unfold your calendar, you will see all the different shapes of the moon.

THREE MOONS?!

Jessica says good night to the moon every night. Tonight something odd has happened.

Can you point to the full moon? Where is the moon in the first quarter? The last quarter? Can you see a new moon?

MOON RIDDLES

Here's a hint: if you have trouble, look back a few pages
to find the answers.

Can you point to what the gardener planted when the moon
was full? Carrots, flowers, lettuce or tomatoes?

In which country would they say that the boy on the left has
"got a bad moon"?

DISCOVERING
SPACE

THE FIRST VOYAGES INTO SPACE

At first we didn't know if a living creature could survive a trip through space. That's why the first to go were dogs and monkeys.

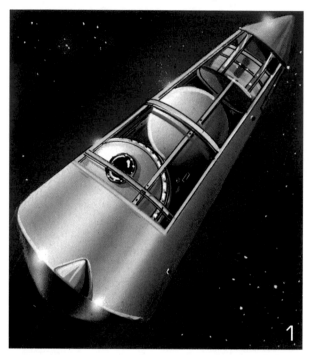

The first living creature to travel in space was a small Russian dog named Laïka (2). She traveled on the first satellite to carry a passenger—Sputnik 2 in 1957 (1). The first woman in space was Russian. She has been around the earth 48 times (3).

Yuri Gagarin

the Vostok spacecraft

John Glenn

The first man in space was a Russian, Yuri Gagarin. He traveled on the Vostok spacecraft. One year later an American, John Glenn, had his turn in space.

THE FIRST TRIP TO THE MOON

More than twenty-five years ago, a team of American astronauts went on a great adventure. This is their story.

NEIL ARMSTRONG

MICHAEL COLLINS

EDWIN ALDRIN

The three astronauts took their places in the Columbia at the tip of the Saturn 5 rocket.

THE SATURN 5 TAKES OFF

Take-off successful! The rocket left the launching pad. It took the astronauts three days to reach the moon.

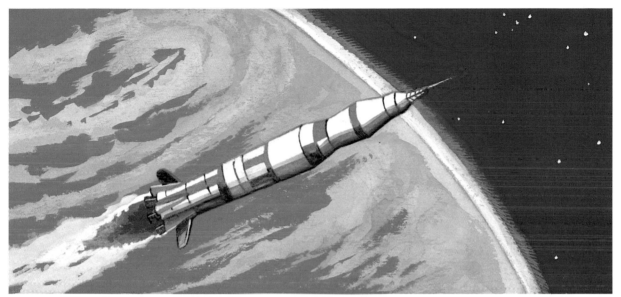

The first two stages of the Saturn 5 rocket fell back to Earth while the last stage continued on to the moon.

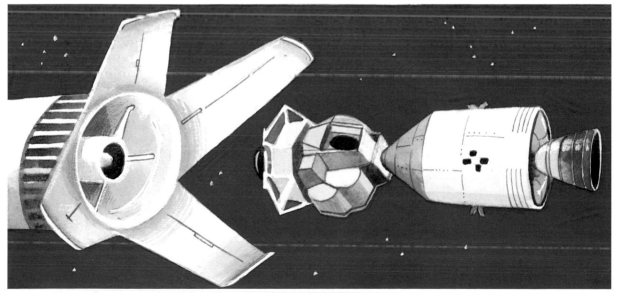

The Columbia separated from the third stage of the rocket and continued on its way towards the moon.

THE LUNAR MODULE

Michael Collins stayed in the Columbia. Neil Armstrong and Edwin Aldrin took their places in a tiny space craft—the lunar module (or LM).

This spacecraft was able to land on the moon and looked like a giant spider.

The lunar module landed on the moon—in a desert called the Sea of Tranquility. Above an astronaut is leaving the lunar module.

THE FIRST WALK ON THE MOON

For the very first time, an astronaut walked on the moon.
Everyone was watching the event on television.

Armstrong climbed out first. Filled with emotion, his first words were: "That's one small step for man. One giant leap for mankind." Aldrin and Armstrong gathered rocks and put measuring instruments in place.

MISSION ACCOMPLISHED!

The lunar module returned to the Columbia and the three astronauts from the Apollo 11 mission returned to Earth.

A parachute slowed their fall and the space capsule landed on the sea. Divers helped the astronauts leave the capsule. They brought back samples of the soil on the moon and moon rocks.

THE LUNAR JEEP

After Apollo 11, several teams of astronauts returned to the moon.
They brought with them a lunar rover!

The astronaut above is carrying cameras to film the landscape in his
jeep. From time to time he stops to gather small moon rocks. Back
on Earth, scientists are waiting to study them.

WORKING ON THE MOON

There isn't any air on the moon so everything is quiet. Astronauts communicate with each other by hand signals or by radio.

Plant a flag or set up an antenna... luckily, astronauts are very light even with their spacesuits on. On the moon everything weighs six times less than on Earth!

WEIGHTLESS IN SPACE

Everything in space is weightless. If you drop something it'll float instead of falling.

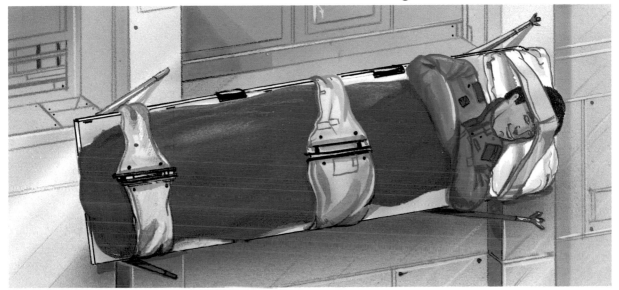

Since everything floats around in a spacecraft, astronauts attach their sleeping bags to the walls.

Astronauts use handholds to move around in their spacecraft.

Before going into space astronauts are trained to live in weightlessness. They practice everything they will have to do.

Astronauts jog on a treadmill to keep in shape.

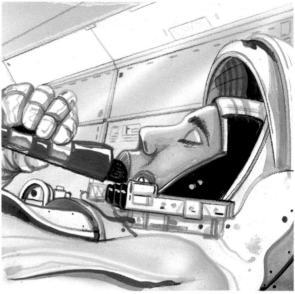

They drink out of a kind of baby bottle so that drops don't float all over the place.

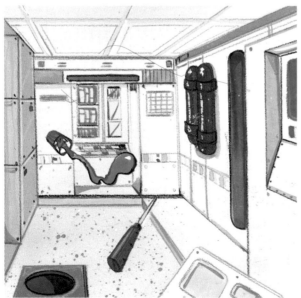

It they aren't attached, all the objects in the cabin float around.

Astronauts know how to repair their own engines.

THE ARIANE ROCKET LAUNCHES SATELLITES

The Ariane rocket is built by Europeans. Below is a drawing of it on its launching pad. The countdown has started.

The cover at the top protects the satellites during take-off.

The third stage releases the satellites 415 miles above the ground.

The second stage drops off 90 miles above the ground.

The first stage drops off 45 miles above the ground.

Huge power tanks burn in order to help the rocket take off.

ARIANE'S VOYAGE

The Ariane rocket drops its stages one by one as it goes up into the sky.
You need a whole new rocket each time you launch a satellite.

Arms and cables fall away.
The engines fire up.

The rocket takes off. The
largest fuel tanks break away.

The first stage falls off and
the second stage is fired up.

The second stage falls off and
the third stage is fired up.

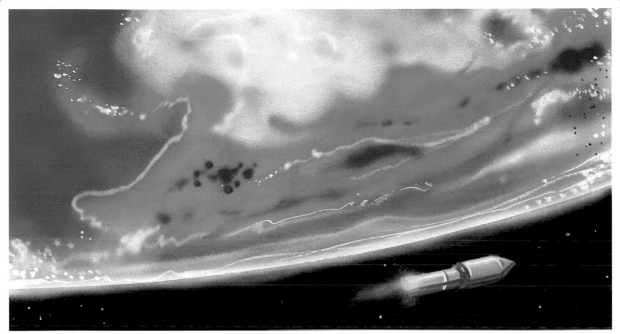

The third stage moves around the earth. It will drop its satellite before reentering the atmosphere and burning up.

The satellite opens its solar panels. When it is in the right place it will send information to Earth.

THE SPACE SHUTTLE

Rockets can only be used once so the United States decided to build a space shuttle.

The space shuttle above is taking off. It is clinging to a huge tank with two propulsors, one on each side. The shuttle will return to Earth.

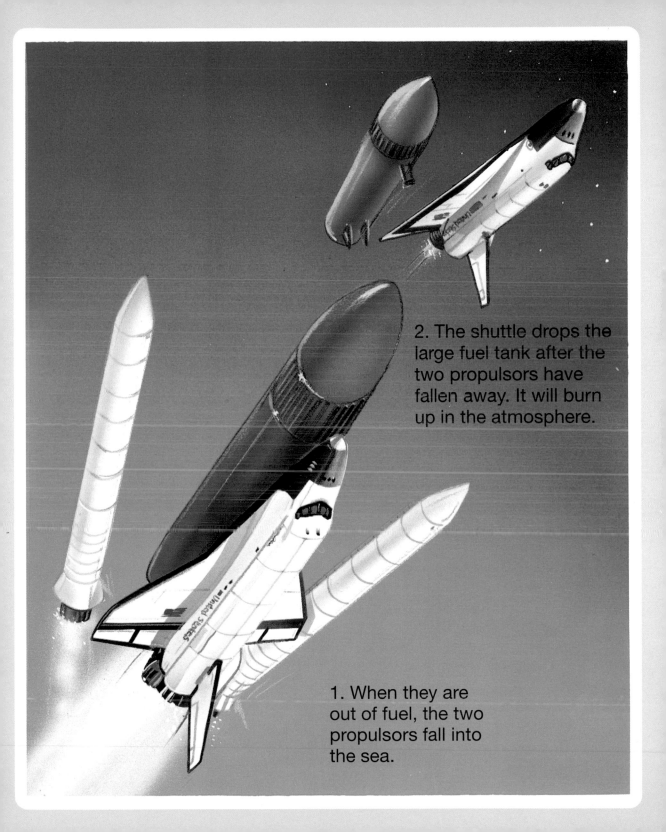

2. The shuttle drops the large fuel tank after the two propulsors have fallen away. It will burn up in the atmosphere.

1. When they are out of fuel, the two propulsors fall into the sea.

THE SHUTTLE'S JOB

The space shuttle flies around Earth. Astronauts drop satellites or pick them up for repairs.

A metal arm comes out of the bay and holds on to the astronauts that leave the shuttle to work in space.

When its mission is accomplished, the shuttle returns to Earth and lands like an airplane. In a little while, it takes off again on a new mission.

MEN WORK IN SPACE

When men first left their spacecraft to work in space they were attached to the cabin by a safety cable.

Now, astronauts have "flying chairs." They can go as far as 100 yards from their spacecraft. They are controlled with joysticks on the arms of the "chairs."

THE SPACE STATION MIR

The space station Mir goes around the earth 16 times a day. Russian cosmonauts take turns in Mir.

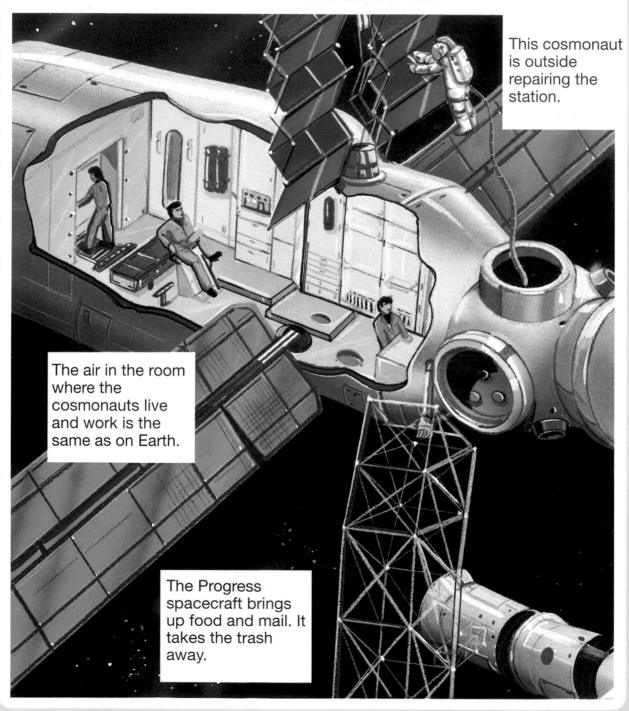

This cosmonaut is outside repairing the station.

The air in the room where the cosmonauts live and work is the same as on Earth.

The Progress spacecraft brings up food and mail. It takes the trash away.

HERMES—THE FIRST EUROPEAN SPACE SHUTTLE

Europeans are getting ready to build the space shuttle Hermes. It will be used to carry the astronauts to the Colombus space station.

The Ariane 5 rocket will carry Hermes into space and drop it there. Hermes will return to Earth like an airplane.

Here is a picture of the future European space station, Colombus. Researchers and technicians will be able to live and work there for a few weeks at a time. Hermes will shuttle back and forth between Earth and Colombus to bring teams up and back.

SPACE PROBES EXPLORE THE UNIVERSE

Space probes are robots that send photos back to Earth.
They are sent to planets that men can't reach yet.

The Mariner 10 probe over Mercury.

The Viking probe landed on Mars. It didn't meet any Martians.

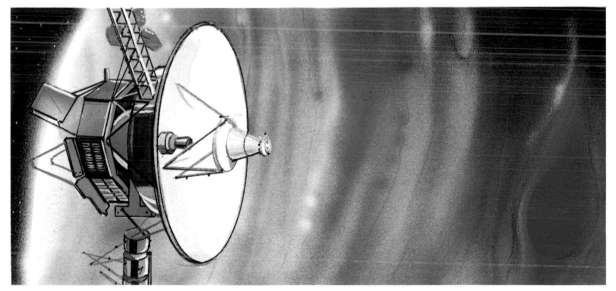

The Voyager space probe flew past Jupiter and Saturn. It will continue on to Neptune and then get lost in outer space.

SATELLITES WORK FOR US

Satellites are very useful tools for us. They let us communicate and help us learn more about the universe.

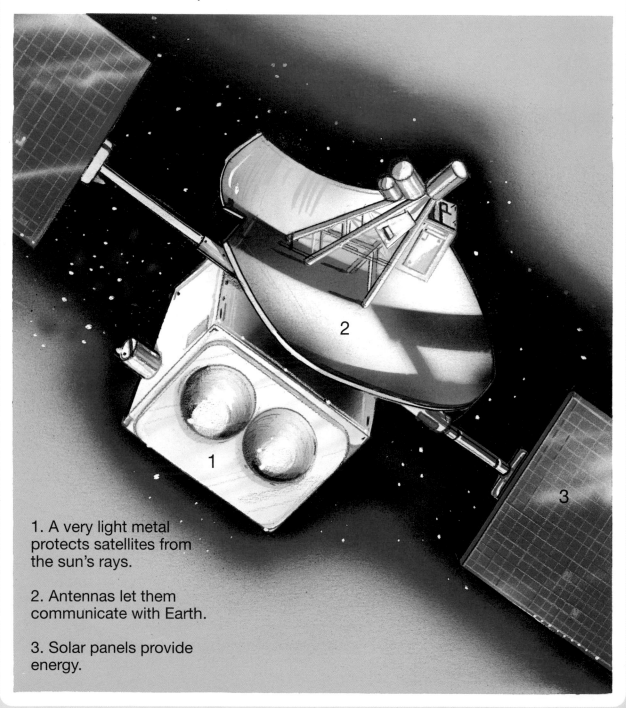

1. A very light metal protects satellites from the sun's rays.

2. Antennas let them communicate with Earth.

3. Solar panels provide energy.

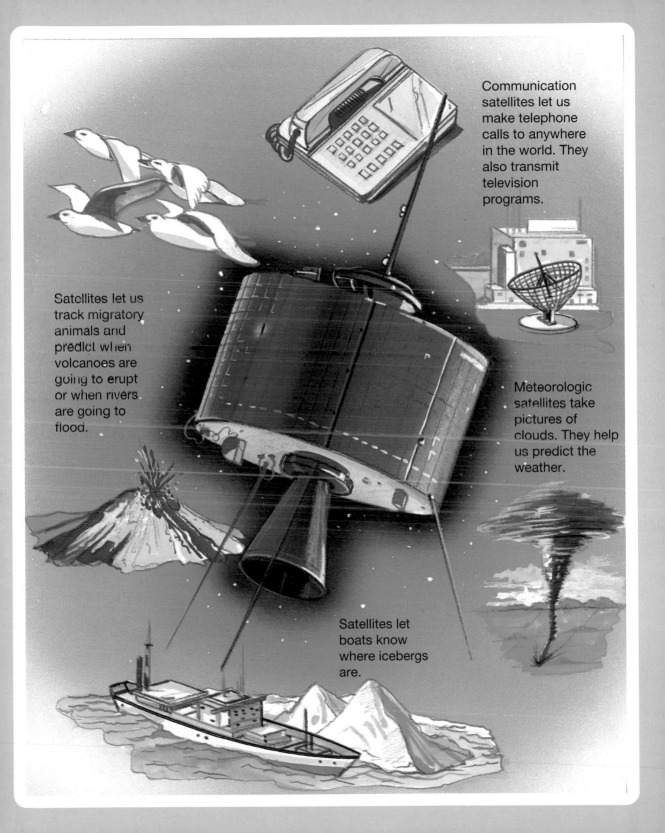

Communication satellites let us make telephone calls to anywhere in the world. They also transmit television programs.

Satellites let us track migratory animals and predict when volcanoes are going to erupt or when rivers are going to flood.

Meteorologic satellites take pictures of clouds. They help us predict the weather.

Satellites let boats know where icebergs are.

A LUNAR BASE CAMP

Scientists have imagined a city on the moon. Houses would be underground. Space shuttles could take off and land at the base.

CITIES IN OUTER SPACE

Thousands of people could live in space. They would make their homes in huge space stations.

THINK CAREFULLY!
What is this rocket going to drop?
Meteorites (1), a satellite (2) or a comet (3)?

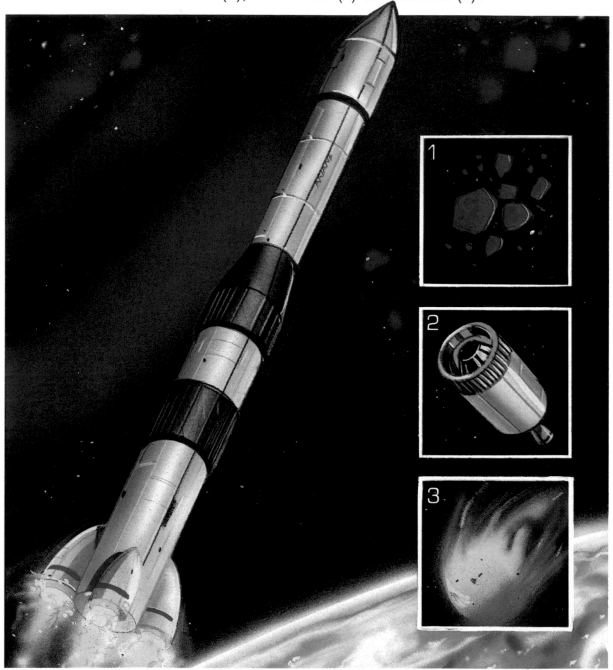

What do rockets do while they travel in space?

LANDING ON MARS

Which of these three machines are going to land on Mars? If you can't remember, look back at the page about space probes.

WHICH ONE?

Look carefully at these machines. Which one is going to return to Earth and land like an airplane? Which one will be destroyed in space?

FUN WITH ALIENS!

Scientists have sent radio messages into space but no one has answered yet!

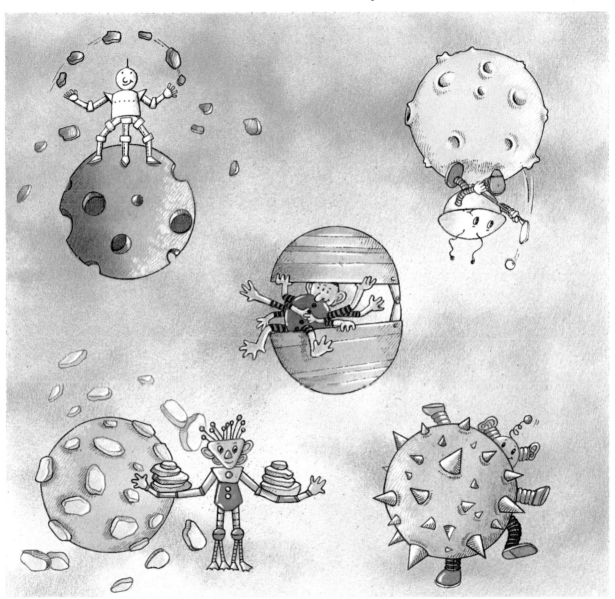

Until we meet aliens, you can imagine them for yourself. What will they be like? Can you point to the alien inside his planet? And the one on top of his planet? Next to it? Behind it? Under it?

MESSAGES FROM SPACE

Astronauts often send radio messages to their children on Earth.
Match each child with his or her dad.

THE RIGHT ROCKET SHIP

Three astronauts have gone into space in their "flying chairs."
Can you help each one find his own rocket?

MAKE A ROCKET CAKE

This rocket cake is easy to make but it takes a long time. Have a grown-up help you follow the instructions below.

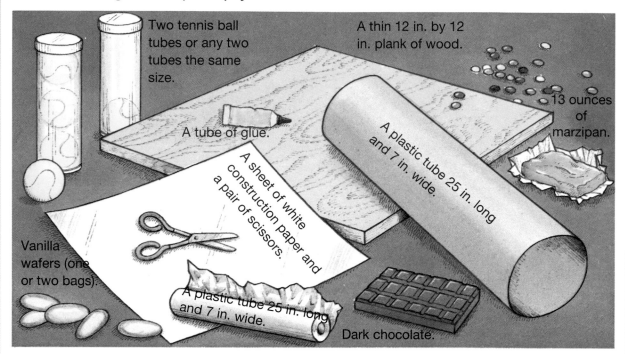

Two tennis ball tubes or any two tubes the same size.

A thin 12 in. by 12 in. plank of wood.

A tube of glue.

A plastic tube 25 in. long and 7 in. wide.

13 ounces of marzipan.

A sheet of white construction paper and a pair of scissors.

Vanilla wafers (one or two bags).

A plastic tube 25 in. long and 7 in. wide.

Dark chocolate.

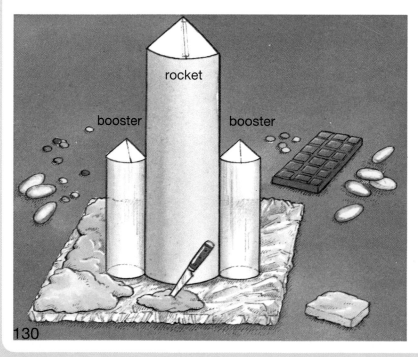

rocket

booster

booster

Glue the rocket and the boosters to the wooden board. Then make three cones out of the construction paper and glue them to the tops of the tubes. Let the glue dry. Cover the board with aluminum foil. Next, spread the marzipan on the aluminum foil.

1. Melt 10 ounces of dark chocolate (add a little bit of water).
2. Spread the melted chocolate on the flat side of the vanilla wafers one by one.
3. Stick them on the rocket and boosters while the chocolate is still soft like in the picture.
4. Dip pieces of hard candy in the chocolate and stick them between the cookies.

This spectacular rocket cake will surprise all your friends!